NEIGHBORHOOD SAFETY
Written by
Susan Kesselring
Illustrated by
Dan McGeehan
I0817175
SAFETY FIRST
LET'S READ
AV2
BY WEIGL™
ADDED VALUE • AUDIO VISUAL
www.av2books.com

Go to **www.av2books.com**, and enter this book's unique code.

BOOK CODE

AVA37727

AV² by Weigl brings you media enhanced books that support active learning.

AV² provides enriched content that supplements and complements this book. Weigl's AV² books strive to create inspired learning and engage young minds in a total learning experience.

Your AV² Media Enhanced books come alive with...

Audio
Listen to sections of the book read aloud.

Video
Watch informative video clips.

Embedded Weblinks
Gain additional information for research.

Try This!
Complete activities and hands-on experiments.

Key Words
Study vocabulary, and complete a matching word activity.

Quizzes
Test your knowledge.

Slide Show
View images and captions, and prepare a presentation.

... and much, much more!

Published by AV² by Weigl
350 5th Avenue, 59th Floor New York, NY 10118
Website: www.av2books.com

Library of Congress Cataloging-in-Publication Data

Names: Kesselring, Susan, author.
Title: Neighborhood Safety / Susan Kesselring.
Other titles: Being safe in your neighborhood
Description: New York, NY : AV² by Weigl, [2020] | Series: Safety First |
Identifiers: LCCN 2018053398 (print) | LCCN 2018056480 (ebook) | ISBN 9781489699695 (Multi User Ebook) | ISBN 9781489699701 (Single User Ebook) | ISBN 9781489699671 (hardcover : alk. paper) | ISBN 9781489699688 (softcover : alk. paper)
Subjects: LCSH: Safety education--Juvenile literature. | Children's accidents--Prevention--Juvenile literature. | Children--Crimes against--Prevention--Juvenile literature.
Classification: LCC HQ770.7 (ebook) | LCC HQ770.7 .K47 2020 (print) | DDC 613.6071--dc23
LC record available at https://lccn.loc.gov/2018053398

Printed in the United States of America in Brainerd, Minnesota
1 2 3 4 5 6 7 8 9 0 22 21 20 19 18

112018
102918

Project Coordinator: Jared Siemens Designer: Ana María Vidal

First published by The Child's World in 2011

In this book, you will learn about

neighborhood safety,

what to do,

what not to do,

and much more!

What is fun to do in your neighborhood? Isn't playing with friends great? Do you ever get a sundae at the ice cream shop? Or do you find cool books at the library?

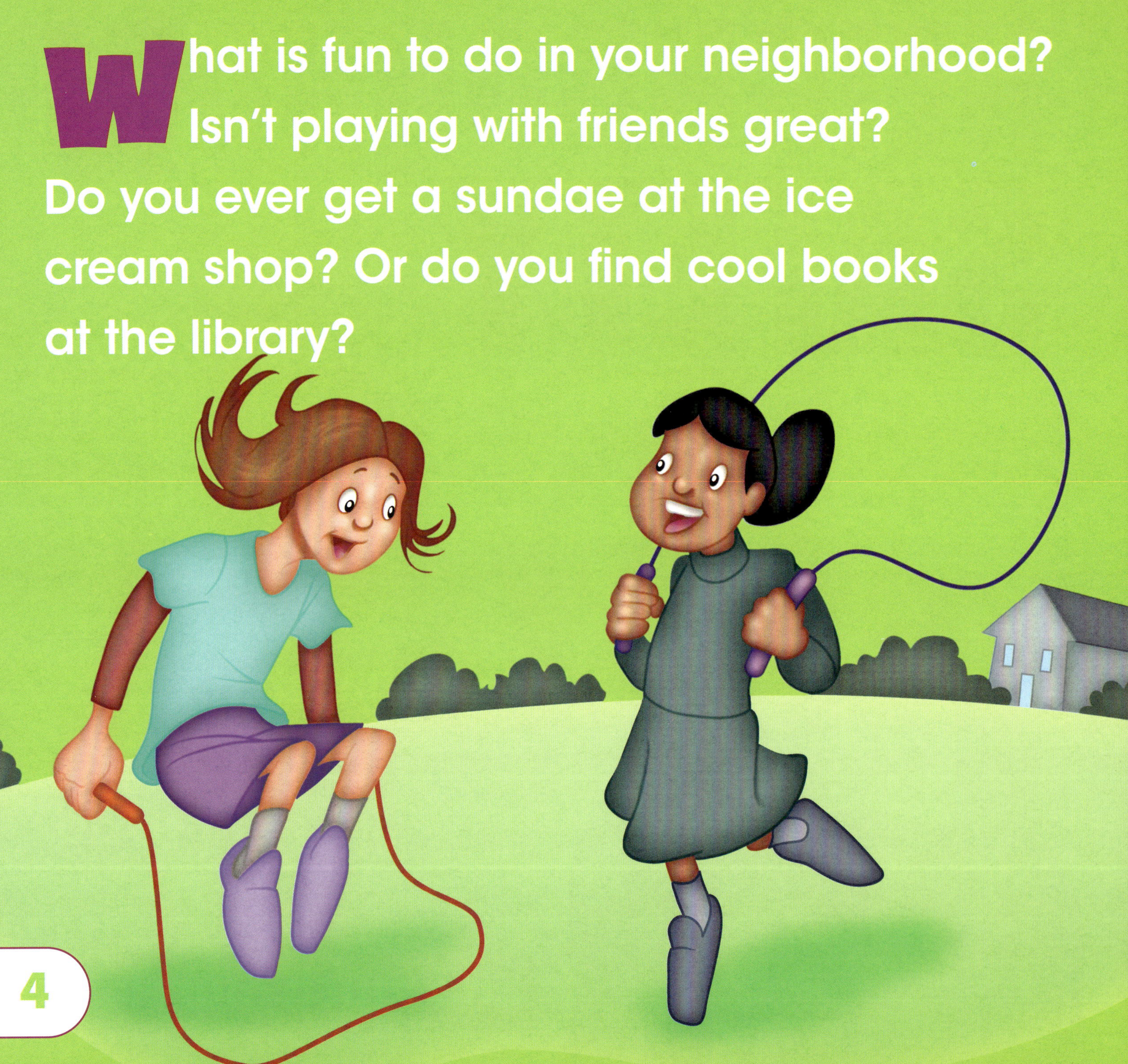

You play in your neighborhood all the time. Learn a few simple rules, and you can have fun and stay safe close to home.

I ♥ MY NEIGHBORHOOD
A crosswalk is a path for people crossing a road. It is usually marked with white lines. Always try to cross a street at a crosswalk.

Does your neighborhood have a lot of streets? You know not to play in the street. But what if you need to cross it to get to your friend's house?

Have an adult help you find a safe place to cross. You should be able to see far away in both directions. Look both ways for cars. When the coast is clear, walk across the street. Keep your head up and your eyes and ears alert for cars.

Are there woods in your neighborhood? A parent will know if it is safe to play there.

If it is safe, stay near the edge of the trees. This way, you can always find your way out. Playing in the woods can be fun, but it is easy to get lost among the trees.

Take a flashlight to the woods. It will help you see if it gets dark. You should also take a whistle. It will help others find you if you get lost.

I ♥ MY NEIGHBORHOOD

It's so fun to watch wild animals in your neighborhood. But avoid feeding squirrels, raccoons, or any other wild guests. Keep your distance, too. These animals need their space.

Stay away from injured and dead animals. Tell an adult about them instead.

If a wild animal bites or scratches you, tell an adult right away. Some animals can give you a disease. You might need to see a doctor.

I ♥ MY NEIGHBORHOOD

Do you love to pet dogs? Just remember to always ask the dog's owner first. The dog might not be safe to touch.

If the owner says it is okay, let the dog smell you first. Then you can pet the dog gently on its chest or under its chin.

Don't get too close to dogs tied outside stores. The dog doesn't know you. It could get scared and bite you.

If you see a stray dog or cat, you might want to help it. Don't get too close or try to catch it. Instead, have a parent call the police or an animal shelter.

If a stray dog runs toward you, don't run away. Instead, act like a tree. Stare straight ahead and be very still. If the dog looks like it might bite you, throw something. The dog will chase after what you threw. Then, run away as fast as you can.

I ♥ MY NEIGHBORHOOD
It is good to know your parents' full names. If you get lost, you can explain for whom you are looking.
MR. + MRS. JO S
123 ELM ST.
PH: 555-1234

It is possible to lose your parents in a crowd or a store. Memorize your address and your parents' phone numbers. Knowing these will help you get home if you are lost.

These numbers might be hard to remember at first. Writing them on a piece of paper can help. Attach the paper to the inside of your backpack or keep it in your pocket.

Stay where you are when you are lost. Look around for your parents. Call out for them too, even if you are somewhere quiet.

If you still cannot find your parents, tell an adult you are lost. Find a police officer, a store worker, or a family to ask for help. Before you know it, you will find your parents!

Stores often have speakers that let them talk to shoppers. A worker can use the speakers to ask your mom or dad to come meet you when you are lost.

I ♥ MY NEIGHBORHOOD

You cannot tell if a person is someone you can trust just by looking at him or her. Be careful!
I ♥ MY NEIGHBORHOOD

When you're lost, strangers can help you. But the rules for strangers are different when it's not an emergency. If a stranger offers you a ride, candy, or gifts, run away. Go home or to a place with other adults.

Never go anywhere with a stranger, even if the stranger says he or she knows your family. And always tell your parents if a stranger bothers you.

Always take a friend with you when you are out in the neighborhood. It is safer than going out alone. You can play together and help each other if you have any problems.

With a neighborhood buddy, you can stay safe and have fun!

KEY WORDS

Research has shown that as much as 65 percent of all written material published in English is made up of 300 words. These 300 words cannot be taught using pictures or learned by sounding them out. They must be recognized by sight. This book contains 134 common sight words to help young readers improve their reading fluency and comprehension. This book also teaches young readers several important content words, such as proper nouns.

Page	Sight Words First Appearance
4	a, at, books, do, find, get, great, in, is, or, the, to, what, with, you, your
5	all, and, be, can, close, few, for, have, home, how, I, learn, me, play, tell, time, watch, will
6	always, it, lines, people, try, white
7	an, away, both, but, cars, does, eyes, far, head, help, house, if, keep, know, look, need, not, of, place, see, should, up, walk, ways, when
9	also, are, near, others, out, take, there, this, trees
11	about, animals, any, from, give, it's, might, right, so, some, their, them, these, too
13	ask, could, don't, first, its, just, let, on, says, then, under
15	after, as, call, like, runs, something, still, very, want
16	good, names
17	hard, numbers, paper
19	around, before, come, even, family, often, talk, that, use, where
20	by, her, him
21	different, go, he, never, she
23	each, than, together

Page	Content Words First Appearance
4	friends, ice cream shop, library, neighborhood, sundae
5	rules
6	crosswalk, path, road, street
7	adult, coast, directions, ears
9	edge, flashlight, parent, whistle, woods
11	disease, doctor, guests, raccoons, space, squirrels
13	chest, chin, dogs, owner, stores
15	animal shelter, cat, police
17	address, backpack, crowd, phone, piece, pocket
19	dad, mom, officer, shoppers, speakers, worker
21	candy, emergency, gifts, ride, strangers
23	buddy, problems